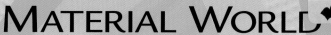

Glass

by Claire Llewellyn

W
FRANKLIN WATTS
LONDON•SYDNEY

This edition 2005
Franklin Watts
96 Leonard Street
London EC2A 4XD

Franklin Watts Australia
Level 17/207 Kent Street
Sydney NSW 2000

Text copyright © Claire Llewellyn 2001

ISBN 0 7496 6230 1

Dewey Classification Number: 666'.1

A CIP catalogue record for this book
is available from the British Library

Series editor: Rosalind Beckman
Series designer: James Evans
Picture research: Sue Mennell
Photography: Steve Shott

Printed in China

Acknowledgements

Thanks are due to the following for kind permission to
reproduce photographs:
The Art Archive p. 7m (Dagli Orti (A))
Corbis Images pp. 9t (Nathan Benn), 10 (Bojan Brecelj),
11t (Robert Holmes, 14 (William James Warren), 15t (digital
image © 1996 Corbis; original image courtesy of NASA),
18b Tom Bean), 19b (Peter Harholdt), 21b (Adam Woolfitt),
26 (James L. Amos)
Ecoscene pp. 8 (Eva Miessler), 17t (Lorenzo Lees), 21t (Gill),
27t (Mike Whittler)
Franklin Watts p. 17b (Chris Fairclough)
Holt Studios p. 13t (Nigel Cattlin)
Pilkington plc pp. 20, 22
Science Photo Library pp. 13b (Adam Hart-Davis), 19t (Peter
Menzel), 24 (Simon Fraser)
Still Pictures pp. 12t (Roland Seitre), 15b (Ron Giling),
18-19 (Mark Edwards), 23b and back cover (Argus), 25b (Mark
Edwards), 27b (Hartmut Schwarzbach)

Thanks are also due to John Lewis for their help with this
project, and to Liberty and Dina Ginsburg for lending items
for photography.

Contents

Words printed in **_bold italic_** are explained in the glossary.

What is glass?

Glass is a beautiful and useful material. It is hard to imagine life without it. It is used in every home, every car and every building.

Made of glass

The most common kind of glass breaks when you drop it and shatters into very sharp pieces. But some kinds of glass are so strong, they are almost impossible to break.

All the things in these pictures are made of glass. Can you name them all?

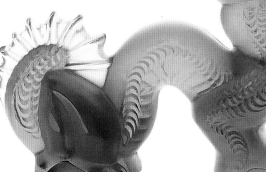

Material words

Which of these words describe glass?

cold   thick   shiny   sticky   stretchy   stiff   solid   heavy   soft   strong   dull   hard   warm   hard-wearing   spongy   light   crisp   colourful   rough   smooth   thin   bendy   slimy   springy   runny   squashy

WARNING

Always take care with glass. If you break it, it is very sharp.

Try this

Collect five different things made of glass. Examine them carefully. Tap them gently with your fingernails. How are they different from one another? How are they the same?

Glass is transparent

We use glass to make windows because it is clear and lets the light shine through. In places where we want less light, we use *tinted* or *frosted* glass instead.

Glass windows

When sunlight streams through the glass windows of a building, it brings light and heat inside. That's why glass is so widely used in countries that have less sun. Greenhouses are made completely of glass. The plants inside get plenty of sunshine, and this helps them to grow.

Plants grow well in a greenhouse. They get plenty of heat and light.

Tinted glass

In buildings where there are many windows, the rooms can sometimes get too hot. Windows made of tinted glass let less sunlight through, helping to keep rooms cool. Tinted glass also cuts down the *glare* of bright sunlight.

Frosted glass

Not all glass is **transparent**. Windows in bathrooms or front doors are often made of frosted glass. It lets some light through but stops people seeing inside.

Many modern skyscrapers have glass walls. This one is made of tinted glass, to cut down the glare of the Sun.

Try this

First, plant two or three beans in some soil in a small plastic pot. Do not cover it. Next, plant two or three beans in a jam jar of soil and put on a screw-top lid. Leave the beans on a window sill for about two weeks. Which beans grow first?

Glass reflects light

When rays of light hit a glass mirror, they bounce back off again. This is called *reflection*. Mirrors are very useful to us. They help in many different ways.

Looking at mirrors

A mirror is made of a flat sheet of glass with a smooth, silver coating on the back. Rays of light bounce off an object in front of the mirror and pass through the glass. The rays then bounce off the silver coating and into your eyes. You can see whatever is reflected.

A clown puts on his make-up with the help of a mirror.

Glass lamps

Glass is often used to make lamps. This is not only because glass is transparent, but also because light looks beautiful as it is reflected off the polished glass. This is especially true of chandeliers, which contain hundreds of pieces of glass.

A chandelier looks sparkly because the light bounces off the specially-cut pieces of glass.

Try this

Take two small mirrors and stand them up to make a corner. Now place an object in the corner and look at it in the two mirrors. How much of the object can you see?

Glass helps us to see

Light 'bends' when it passes through glass, and this changes the way we see things. Many *lenses* are made of glass. They make things look bigger or sharper.

How light bends

When rays of light pass through glass, they slow down a little and change direction. This makes the light look as if it is 'bending' and changes the way we see things.

The lenses in binoculars allow us to see things that are a long way away.

Try this

Hold a pencil behind a thick glass object so that half the pencil is above it and half is below. Now stand back and look at the pencil. Do you notice anything strange about it?

Using lenses

Lenses are made of glass and other transparent materials. They are carefully shaped so that they will 'bend' the light in different ways. They are often used in scientific instruments. The lenses inside a microscope make tiny things look bigger.

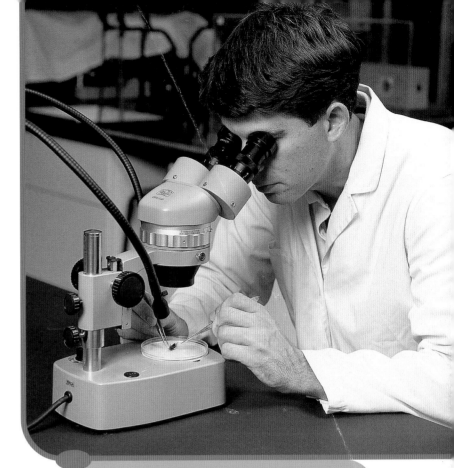

This scientist is using a microscope to study an insect more closely.

Seeing clearly

People have worn glass lenses for hundreds of years. Today, most lenses are made of plastic, which is lighter to wear and cheaper to produce.

Eye experts, called optometrists, test people's eyes by trying out different lenses. These special lenses are made of glass.

Glass is strong

Some kinds of glass are very hard and strong, and difficult to break. They stand up to hard wear, great heat and years of bad weather.

This car windscreen is still holding together even though the glass is broken.

Taking hard wear

Car windscreens are made of two sheets of glass with a layer of plastic in the middle. The glass is so tough that it rarely breaks when stones fly up and hit it. If it does break, the bits of glass stick to the plastic and do not fly through the air.

Taking the heat

Ordinary glass breaks when it is heated or cooled, but some kinds of glass do not. *Heatproof* glass can stand such high temperatures that it is used to make dishes for cooking.

Spacecraft windows are made of special glass that can stand the extremely cold temperatures in space.

The modern glass entrance to the Louvre Museum in Paris is as hard-wearing as the old stone buildings nearby.

Taking the weather

Modern buildings contain a lot of glass - not only in the windows but also in the roofs and outer walls. The glass stands up to the weather for many years without breaking or growing dull.

Fantastic fact

Some glass is so strong that it can be carved like stone. It is known as cut glass.

Glass keeps things clean

Glass helps to keep things clean in offices, schools and homes. Food containers are often made of glass because it is clean and safe to use.

A glass barrier

A piece of glass keeps out dirt and dust. The glass in picture frames protects photographs and can easily be cleaned. Glass covers the faces of watches and clocks to protect their delicate hands.

Glass containers

Glass is often used to make bottles and jars. Glass has no smell or taste, so it is a good material for storing food and drink. Many glass containers have screw tops. These seal the jars tightly and help to keep food fresh.

Glass jars are useful for storing food. It's easy to see what each jar holds and how much you have left.

Drinking from glass

Glass is such a clean material that it is used to make drinking glasses. Many soft drinks are sold in glass bottles. The glass needs to be quite thick so that the bottles can be carried without breaking.

Try this

Take a glass and a plastic cup and fill them with water. Now drink from each one. How does each one feel against your lips?

Glass is made from sand and rocks

Glass is made by heating sand and rocks. A natural kind of glass is made by **volcanoes** and lightning, but the glass we use is made in factories.

Made by volcanoes

Before people learned to make glass, they found it in the world around them. The heat from volcanoes melts rock and sand. This sometimes forms a hard glass called **obsidian**. People used it long ago to make arrowheads and knives.

A *limestone quarry* - limestone is one of the *raw materials* used for making glass.

Long ago people used obsidian to make arrowheads, which could then be used for hunting.

18

Made by lightning

During thunderstorms, hot flashes of lightning shoot to the ground. If they strike sand, the grains melt to form long, glassy tubes called *fulgurites*. The tubes harden as they cool but are easy to break.

Thin glass fulgurites are too fragile to use.

Made by people

Most glass is made from three raw materials - sand, limestone and soda ash - which are widely found in the ground. The rocks are dug out of quarries or mines, and ground up into a powder. They are then taken to a *glassworks*.

Fantastic fact

These bottles and jugs were made by the Romans about 2,000 years ago.

Making glass

Glass is made by melting the sand and rocks, and leaving them to cool. The glass can be treated in different ways to produce coloured, heatproof or other kinds of glass.

The basic recipe

A basic recipe is used to make ordinary glass. The raw materials are weighed and mixed, and then poured into a *furnace*. Here, they melt into a thick syrup that hardens into glass as it cools.

Inside the furnace the sand and rocks melt into a runny liquid.

Changing the colour

Changing the basic recipe produces different types of glass. Adding metals to the mixture changes the colour of the glass. Yellow, blue or red glass can be made by adding silver, copper or gold.

People still practise the ancient art of making stained-glass windows. They use small pieces of coloured glass to make modern designs.

Re-heating the glass after shaping helps to make it tougher.

Changing the glass

Different materials can be added early in production to make glass stronger or more heatproof. Sometimes the glass is treated later in production. Re-heating the glass and then cooling it quickly makes it up to four times stronger.

Fantastic fact

A furnace in a glassworks never stops working. It may carry on burning for ten years, until its walls wear out.

Shaping glass

Hot melted glass is easy to shape.
The shaping can be done in different ways.
Sometimes the glass is shaped by hand,
but usually it is shaped by machine.

This glass sheet was made by floating melted glass on a bath of melted tin.

Shaping by machine

Glass is shaped to make all sorts of things. It can be pressed into a **mould** to make cooking dishes, or blown into moulds to make bottles and light bulbs. Window glass is made by pouring the runny glass on to a bath of melted tin. The glass floats on top of the tin, where it cools to make a smooth sheet of glass.

Shaping by hand

Craftsmen and women have always used glass to make beautiful things for the home. They usually prefer to shape the glass by hand. They put a blob of soft glass on to the end of a blowpipe and blow it into a bubble. Then they shape the glass bubble before it cools.

Glass-blowing takes a lot of skill as the glass must be shaped quickly before it cools.

Fantastic fact

The first light bulbs were hand blown. Now they are made on machines that produce 66,000 an hour.

Saving glass

In many parts of the world glass is being wasted, and more sand and rocks are being dug out of the ground. We need to use glass more carefully, and **recycle** it instead of throwing it away.

Too much glass

In many countries, people use too much glass.

A lot of glass is used to make bottles and jars that are simply thrown away. Throwing away glass is not just a waste in itself. It is also a waste of the materials and **energy** that were used to produce it.

Throwing away glass is a waste. It can easily be recycled.

Re-use and recycle

One way to save glass is by re-using it. Glass does not spoil with age and can be used over and over again. In some places, beer, wine, fizzy drink and milk bottles are collected and re-used.

The glass that we recycle is used to make new glass bottles like these.

At the bottle banks, the glass is sorted by colour: clear, brown or green.

Waste glass can also be recycled. In many parts of the world there are collection centres, called bottle banks, where people take empty bottles and jars. These are taken to a glassworks where they are made into brand new glass.

Fantastic fact

It takes around 3,000 bottles to fill a bottle bank.

Recycling glass

Glass can be recycled over and over again and will always make perfect glass. Recycling saves energy and raw materials, and is good for the **environment**.

New glass for old

At the glassworks, the old glass is cleaned and crushed into tiny pieces called **cullet**. The cullet is mixed with a little new sand, limestone and soda ash, and melted to make new glass. Cullet melts much more easily than the raw materials, and so less energy is used.

Recycled glass is made mostly from crushed glass, which is known as cullet.

These workers are sorting through broken glass at a recycling plant. Recycling glass is a way of saving energy.

Helping the environment

If we recycle old glass, we use fewer raw materials. We do not spoil our environment with quarries and mines, and we save the energy that is needed to work them. Glass jars that are thrown away in the dustbin are buried in *landfill sites*. Recycling stops us filling these places with a material that will not rot.

Most of the bottles and jars we buy every day are made of recycled glass.

Fantastic fact

About one-tenth of all our rubbish is made of glass.

Glossary

Cullet   Old glass that has been crushed ready for recycling.

Energy   The power that makes machines and living things able to work.

Environment   The world around us, including the land, the air and the sea.

Frosted   Glass that has a pattern on it, which makes it difficult to see through.

Fulgurite   Thin glass that is made when lightning melts sand.

Furnace   A very hot oven that is used in factories, such as glassworks.

Glare   Dazzling sunlight.

Glassworks   A factory where glass is made.

Heatproof   Able to stand up to great heat without breaking.

Landfill site   A place where rubbish is buried.

Lens   A piece of glass or transparent plastic that has been specially shaped so that it changes the way we see things.

Limestone	A kind of rock.
Mould	A container with a special shape. Glass can be pushed into a mould to take on its shape.
Obsidian	A hard glass that is made by volcanoes.
Quarry	A place where rocks are dug out of the ground.
Raw materials	The natural materials that are used to make something new.
Recycle	To take an object or material and use it to make something else.
Reflection	The way light bounces off something and into our eyes.
Tinted	Glass that has had colour added to it. Tinted glass lets less sunlight through.
Transparent	Clear or see-through.
Volcano	A crack in the surface of the Earth through which red-hot rock and ash sometimes explode. In time, this builds up to form a mountain.

Index